Author Biogra

CW01509043

Say hello to Nicole Soham, a special fı　　　　　　 ...ugıcs anu a big dreamer!

When she was little she had one big dream: to have a budgie to play with. It only happened after she had already grown up, but now she is living her dream: surrounded by her feathery friends, playing, dancing and having the best times together!

Nicole hopes that you adore your little budgie(s) as much as she adores hers. She is over the moon excited to share her love for budgies with you through this amazing book.

During this wonderful journey filled with fun, learning, laughter and adventure, you'll discover the secrets of caring for your budgie, from setting up a cosy home, to teaching tricks and creating a bedtime routine to having exciting adventures together.

But that's not all! You may wonder if budgies dream and what they might dream about. Isn't that an intriguing question?

Ready for take-off, my dear friends? Then join Nicole on this incredible budgie adventure! Together, let's explore the wonder of having a budgie friend and create beautiful memories that will make your hearts flutter with joy.

Now, let the magic of these words and the many beautiful colour-in pictures carry you away into the enchanting world of budgies. Choosing your own unique colours for the budgies in this book will make the book even more special to you.

Enjoy every page, giggle with delight, and cherish the special bond you share with your own budgie friend.

With love and feathers,

Nicole Soham

Index

Author Biography 1

Chapter 1 Meet My Budgie 7

Chapter 2 Choosing a Budgie 13

Chapter 3 Making Budgie's Home Comfy 17

Chapter 4 Making Fun Toys for My Budgie 21

Chapter 5 Budgie's favourite Foods 27

Chapter 6 Budgie Loves Being Healthy 35

Chapter 7 Budgie Loves Budgie School 41

Chapter 8 Teaching Budgie Cool Tricks 49

Chapter 9 Budgie's Chirpy Talks 53

Chapter 10 Budgie Loves to DANCE 59

Chapter 11 Budgie's Social Life 65

Chapter 12 Adventures with My Budgie 71

Chapter 13 Goodnight Budgie 77

Final Chapter Does My Budgie Dream? 82

Appendix Things I do for My Budgie Every Day 85

What Did You Think of My Budgie Loves to Dance?........... 87

A Little Budgie Song
(in place of a foreword)

A guide for budgies, beyond compare,
Helps you to show your love and care.
Learn the secrets, oh so fine,
To keep your budgie's life divine.
From cage set-up to toys that please,
Watch your budgie thrive with ease.
From proper food to cosy nests,
This guide will help you be the best.
Healthy habits and joyous days,
Guiding your budgie in countless ways.
So open the guide, let knowledge unfurl,
Embrace the bond with your budgie, my pearl.
With this precious handbook by your side,
Together, you'll soar on a joyful ride.

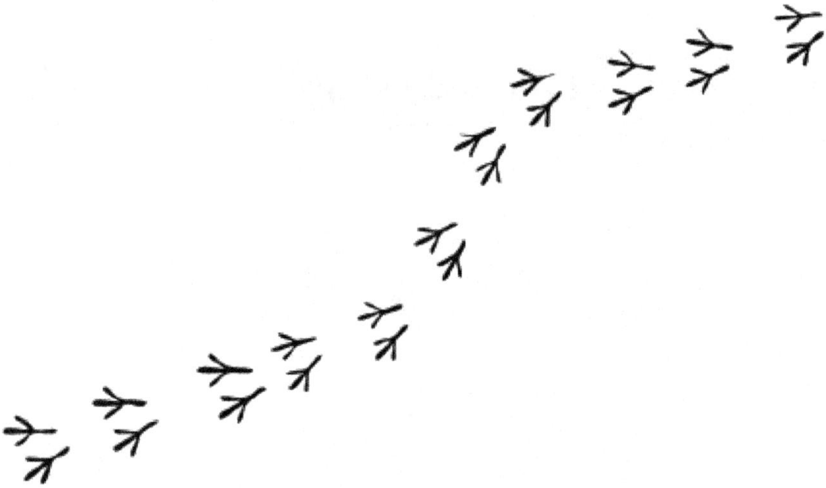

Chapter 1

Meet My Budgie

Why Budgies Are Awesome

Hello, friends!

Welcome to the exciting world of budgies!

Let me introduce you to one of my many feathered friends – a budgie boy, called "Happy"! Happy thinks that budgies are super cute and full of charm.

They are little colourful birds also known as "budgerigars" or just "budgies" for short.

Budgies, are sometimes called parakeets. They make fantastic pets and that's why they are so popular.

But hey, something has happened: My little "Happy" looks so sad!

Little Happy, once so bright,

Lost his colours, what a sight!

But fear not, kids, you hold the key,

Find rainbow colours, set him free!

With colours bold, from red to blue

Paint him happy, it's up to you!

Grab your crayons, let's begin,

Get Happy coloured, let love win!

Fun Fact 1

Colourful Feathers: Budgies come in many dazzling colours, like bright blue, cheerful yellow, lovely green, grey (like my budgie girl Nibbles!) and even fancy combinations of colours.

It's like having a rainbow in your own home! Their personalities are colourful too.

Fun Fact 2

Budgies are super smart! They can learn to do all sorts of amazing things, like mimicking sounds and even talking. They love to show off their clever tricks.

Fun Fact 3

Social Butterflies: Budgies are super social birds. They love being part of a flock and having friends to play with (humans and birds!). If you have more than one budgie, you'll see them having a great time together.

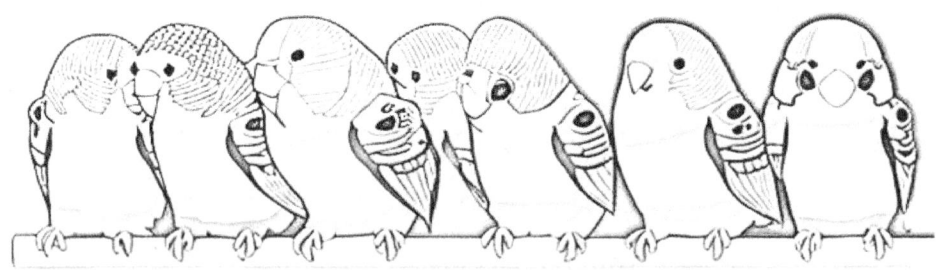

Fun Fact 4

Speaking of chirping, budgies have a language of their own! These tiny birds are big chatterboxes! They use different sounds and melodies to chat with each other and with their human friends. It's like they have their own secret bird code! Listen closely, and you might even hear them say a few words.

Fun Fact 5

Happy Dancers: Ah, here comes the best part – budgie dancing! They love music and will sway, bob, and wiggle their little bodies to the beat. Dancing with my budgie is the best way to brighten my day!

Join in for a budgie boogie?

Fun Fact 6

Budgies have a unique feature called a cere. It's a small patch on their face, just on top of their beak to be exact, that can be blue or pink, depending on whether they are a boy or a girl. Isn't that interesting? Their cere changes over time, with age and with season. In a grown up budgie, a blue cere shows it's a male. A female budgie has a white cere.

Fun Fact 7

Clever Minds: Budgies are smart little thinkers! They can learn all sorts of tricks and games, like ringing a tiny bell or flying through hoops. Teaching them new things is so much fun!

Fun Fact 8

Guess what? Budgies are excellent imitators. They can learn to copy the sounds they hear around them, like the ring of a telephone or even the sound of your laughter. It's like having a feathered comedian in your home!

Fun Fact 9

Special Treats: One of the budgie's favourite things is eating. They enjoy munching on tasty seeds, delicious fruits, and yummy veggies. Offering them a healthy diet keeps them happy and healthy.

Fun Fact 10

Soft Sleepers: When it's bedtime, budgies like to snuggle up and sleep in a cosy, safe spot.

They cover their eyes with their soft feathers, just like a fluffy sleep mask!

Budgies are early birds, just like you should be for school! They wake up early and go to bed at sunset. So, you and your budgie can have a fantastic morning routine together.

Fun Fact 11

Budgies have super special feet! Just like all parrots, their feet have four toes – two in the front and two in the back. That's right, it's like they have tiny birdy hands!

This makes budgies fantastic climbers. They can easily hop and jump around their homes, climbing on different things like little acrobats! And you know what else? They absolutely love hanging upside down. It's like a fun game for them!

So next time you see a budgie, maybe you'll catch them doing some impressive upside-down stunts! Budgies are the little acrobats of the bird world!

These playful little creatures love toys and games, especially ones they can swing on, climb through, or even chew.

Can you build your budgie a tiny amusement park with branches and bird safe toys?

Well, we talk about how to make these a bit later.

Throughout this book you will keep exploring and learning about our feathered friends. Who knows what other fun facts you'll discover?!

Last but not least, budgies can live for a long time if they are well taken care of, bringing joy and laughter to our lives for many years.

That's it for now, my friends! I hope you enjoyed getting to know my budgie and learning these fun facts about these delightful little birds.

Stay tuned for more exciting adventures with budgies in the next chapter!

Chapter 2

Choosing a Budgie with a Brave Heart

Making a Difference

Did you know that there are special budgies out there who have had amazing adventures? These brave budgies have been through exciting journeys and faced challenges in their lives.

Instead of buying a bird from a store, you might consider adopting one of these incredible budgies from a bird rescue.

Let's find out why it's such a great idea!

By adopting a budgie from a bird rescue, you are giving a home to a budgie in need. These special budgies may have had tough times in the past, but with your love and care, you can give them a fresh start and a safe and a caring forever home.

Unconditional Love

Rescue budgies have hearts filled with gratitude. When you adopt a budgie from a bird rescue, they know that you've chosen them and that you're giving them a chance to be part of your family. In return, they'll shower you with love, affection, and endless chirps of joy!

Stories to Share

Every budgie has a unique tale to tell. The budgies in bird rescues may have stories of courage, adventure, and survival. As you build a bond with your adopted budgie, you can discover their amazing history and share their tale with others.

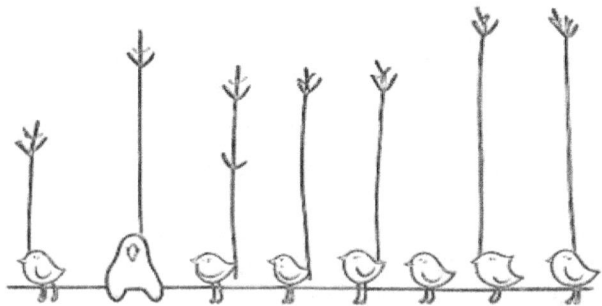

It's like having a feathered superhero in your home!

Making a Positive Impact

By adopting a budgie from a bird rescue, you can help to support the rescue's mission. These organizations work tirelessly to save and care for birds in need.

Your decision to adopt not only brings joy to your home but also helps create a better world for budgies everywhere.

The bird rescue can give you more good information about how to take care of your budgie and make their life a happy one again.

In summary, choosing to adopt a budgie from a bird rescue is a wonderful and compassionate choice. You'll not only give a loving home to a brave budgie but also gain a loyal and extraordinary feathered friend.

So, open your heart and consider the amazing adventure of adopting a budgie with a brave heart!

Chapter 3

Making Budgie's Home Comfy

Choosing a Cage

When it comes to finding a cosy home for your budgie, you want to pick a cage that's just right! Look for a cage that is big enough for your budgie to fly and hop around.

It should have sturdy bars with no chips and a door that's easy to open. Oh, and don't forget to find colourful toys and natural perches for your budgie to play and rest on! More about this in the next chapter.

Setting Up the Cage

Time to make the cage cosy and comfortable for your budgie!

Start by adding soft bedding at the bottom of the cage. You can use paper or special cage liners. Then, place some branches or natural perches of different widths inside for your budgie to sit on.

Budgies love to climb and explore, so add different levels for them to hop around.

Make sure to place their food and water bowls in easily accessible spots too but not underneath the branches, so they stay clean from droppings!

Put the cage in an area that is free from drafts, and is quiet enough for the budgie to relax. And it should be in a spot where they can feel part of the family.

How about near your desk where you study? Or in a corner of your room where they can look out of the window? They need to be able to retreat to have some quiet space when they want to.

One side of the cage could be near a wall or have a cloth hung over it, so budgie can feel safe. This is especially important if budgie is in a new home.

Providing Food and Water

Hungry budgies are not happy budgies, so let's make sure they have plenty to eat and drink!

Fill their food bowl with a mix of yummy seeds and pellets specially made for budgies. You can best find these at a pet shop. Give them only enough for them to nibble on for a day.

I feed my budgies twice a day with fresh food: in the morning, and in the afternoon.

Feeding time is one of the happiest times of the day for my budgies!

Fresh fruits and veggies are great for their health, so give them some small, fresh pieces to munch on.

And don't forget about water!

Change it every day and make sure it's clean and fresh.

We talk much more about what foods are right for your budgie in one of the next chapters, so you can become a great chef for your budgie.

As they say: Food is love!

Creating a Cosy Nesting Area

If you have a boy and a girl budgie and you want them to have baby budgies, you can create a cosy nesting area in their cage.

Place a small nesting box inside the cage, where they can build their nest and lay eggs. Make sure it's a private and quiet spot for them to feel safe and secure.

But remember, taking care of baby budgies requires lots of responsibility and knowledge!

By making your budgie's home comfy, you're giving them a safe and happy place to live. They'll have a cosy spot to sleep, delicious food to eat, and plenty of toys and perches to play with.

Now your budgie will feel right at home and ready to have fun with you!

In the next chapter, we'll explore the wonderful world of budgie toys and activities that will keep your feathered friend entertained and happy. Happy budgie caring!

Chapter 4

Making Fun Toys for My Budgie

Did you know you can make toys for your budgie? It's so much fun, and your feathered friend will love it! But remember, safety comes first.

Each time you introduce a new toy to budgie, allow them to get used to it first. They may at first be afraid of objects they don't know, but over time they'll get curious. In their own time they will want to find out what this new toy is all about.

Do you want some fun ideas for making some safe and exciting toys for your budgie?

Here are some to get you started:

Weaving with Safe Vines and Grasses

Ask an adult for help to find safe vines and grasses that budgies can play with. Avoid using sharp or thorny plants, as they can hurt your budgie.

Soft sea-grass mats are a great option too! Take some of these safe materials and weave them together to make a cool plaything. Your budgie will enjoy climbing and nibbling on this natural toy!

Colourful Paper and Cardboard

Get some colourful, non-toxic paper and cardboard from the craft store. Cut them into fun shapes like circles, triangles, and squares. Punch a tiny hole in each shape and use a safe, non-toxic string to thread them together (long soft grasses will work if you twine them!). Hang this colourful garland in your budgie's cage, and watch them have a blast flying around and pecking at the shapes!

Bells and Beads

Find small, bird-safe bells and beads that don't have any sharp edges and budgies beak or feet can't get stuck in.

Thread them onto a thin, budgie-safe string or leather cord. Tie a knot at each end to secure the bells and beads. Now, you have a jingly toy that your budgie can ring and shake!

Wood Blocks

Ask an adult to help you find safe wood blocks that are free from harmful chemicals. Drill a small hole through each block and thread them onto a safe rope. Tie knots at each end to keep the blocks in place. Your budgie will love to chew and play with these wooden delights!

Safety First

What is the most important thing when making toys for your budgie? That's right: your budgie's safety. Always use materials that are safe for birds. Avoid anything with sharp edges or harmful chemicals or colours.

And here's a bonus tip: rotate the toys in your budgie's cage to keep them entertained with something new every now and then!

Creating toys for your budgie is a wonderful way to show them love and care.

When your budgie plays happily with the toys you made, you'll feel like a true bird toy inventor!

Just remember, if you're ever unsure about whether something is safe for your budgie, always ask an adult for help.

Now, it's time to get creative and make some awesome toys for your budgie buddy!

Have a blast, and enjoy seeing your budgie's excitement as your budgie plays with the toys you've made!

In the next chapter we'll learn what foods budgie likes and how to feed them to keep them healthy and happy.

A Puzzling Little Poem

(to brighten your day)

Who is hanging upside down?
On one foot: a cheerful clown!

A feathered stunt, full of delight,
Spreading fun, oh what a sight!

Upside down, a joyful act
Full of antics - that's a fact!

Is it a bat? Is it a sloth?
A monkey or a sleeping moth?

Swinging freely, full of cheek
It's our budgie "Chatty Beak"!

Chapter 5

Budgie's favourite Foods

Budgies, just like us, need yummy and nutritious food to stay healthy and happy! Let's explore some of their favourite foods together:

Healthy Budgie Seeds and Pellets

Budgies enjoy munching on special seeds and pellets for budgies, but moderation is key!

Offer only enough food for your budgie to nibble on in a day, so you can see if they are happy and eating well. On average, around one to two spoonfuls of seeds daily, depending on their size, is suitable.

You can also make their food healthier by sprouting some seeds. Soaking them in water overnight and rinsing them a few times a day will do the trick. Then let them dry off a little before giving them to your budgie.

It's best not to give them too much dry seed to ensure they stay fit and healthy! Eating dry seeds all the time is like eating popcorn every day.

Fresh Fruits and Vegetables

Just like we enjoy fresh and colourful fruits and vegetables, budgies love them too! It's a tasty and healthy treat for them.

Find out what vegetables your budgie likes. Is it spinach? How about some dandelion leaves, little budgie? Or do you prefer Bok Choi?

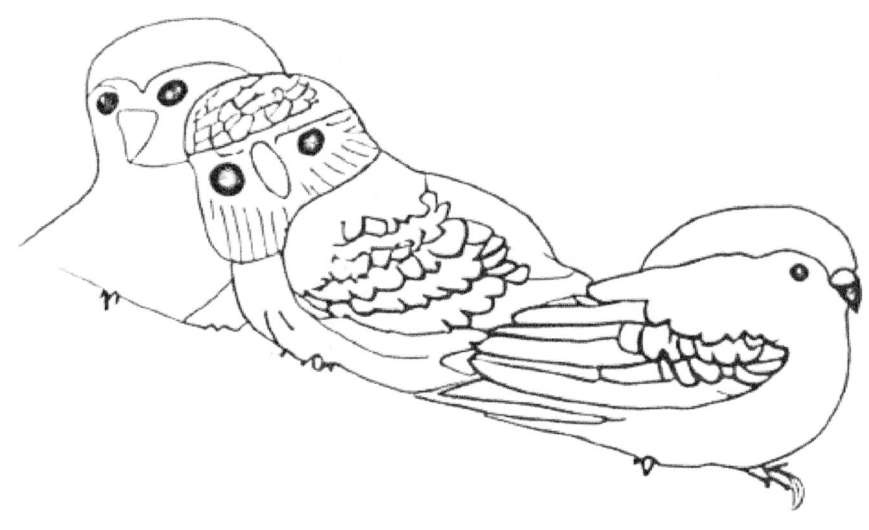

Veggies like spinach, kale, or even some carrot shreds can be great options too! Let's make a rainbow of vegetables!

You can sometimes offer small pieces of fruit like apple, pear, or berries.

Experiment and see which ones make their little beaks go wild with excitement.

Caution: Some vegetables and foods that humans can eat are *very* toxic for budgies. If your budgie eats them they may die. Never give your budgie avocado or anything with chocolate or chocolate flavour, not even very small amounts!

Fresh grass seeds

Did you know that in nature budgies are grass eaters?

Yes, they are an Australian parrot. In Australia, when they live in the wild, budgies eat Kangaroo grass and other Australian native grasses when they are in seed. And they also eat some other green plants (herbs) and even flowers!

So, to make your budgie really happy, you can find some seeding grasses and give them fresh grass with seeds on them.

As we know already, budgies are such awesome pets for people. That's why now they live all over the world in people's homes.

Therefore, if you don't live in Australia and are reading this book, you can find some grasses that grow around where you live and find those that have seeds on them.

Try if your budgie likes to have a nibble! Some budgies will even eat Dandelion flowers.

Giving your budgie fresh seeds from grasses is like bringing a taste of their natural habitat right to their beaks!

Treats and Snacks

Everyone deserves a treat once in a while, and your budgie is no exception! You can find budgie treats at the pet store that are safe for them to enjoy. But remember, treats should be given in moderation. Just like us, budgies need to have a balanced diet.

So save the treats for special occasions or as rewards when you're teaching them tricks or spending quality time together.

Bonus Tip

A nice, occasional treat for budgies is millet spray. You can use these treats to teach your budgie some fun tricks.

We will learn more about teaching your budgie tricks soon!

By giving your budgie a variety of healthy foods every day, you're making them strong and vibrant. Budgies need a balanced diet with a mix of seeds pellets, fresh fruits, vegetables, and occasional treats.

So, let's feed our budgie friends the good stuff and see them chirp with delight!

Now that we know what foods budgies love, it's time to create a colourful and nutritious meal plan for our feathered buddies. Are you ready to become a budgie chef and provide them with delicious and healthy treats?

Let's get cooking!

If you have any questions or want more ideas about budgie's favourite foods, don't hesitate to ask an adult or do some research together.

Happy feeding, and enjoy watching your budgie enjoy their scrumptious meals!

Check out this interesting table! It tells us which foods you can eat and which ones your budgie can eat. Remember, budgies are birds. They have a different tummy! That's why only some foods we eat are also safe for them.

If there's a ✓ , it means it's safe to eat, but if you see a ✕ ✕ ✕ , it's not safe to eat. Can you discover foods your little budgie friend can eat but you should not?

Foods	Children can eat	Budgies can eat
Apples	✓	✓
Avocado	✓	✕ ✕ ✕
Blueberries	✓	✓
Broccoli	✓	✓
Carrots	✓	✓
Chocolate	✓	✕ ✕ ✕
Celery	✓	✓
Banana	✓	✓
Dandelion leaves/flowers*	✓	✓
Grapes	✓	✓
Kangaroo Grass*	✕ ✕ ✕	✓
Pear	✓	✓
Green Beans	✓	✓
Milk and Milk Products	✓	✕ ✕ ✕
Spinach	✓	✓
Sprouted Seeds	✓	✓
Strawberries	✓	✓
Small amounts of grass*	✕ ✕ ✕	✓
Watermelon	✓	✓

*make sure any foods gathered outside have not been sprayed with toxins

Chapter 6

Budgie Loves Being Healthy

Budgies are little champions when it comes to staying healthy and strong. Let's learn how we can keep our feathered friends happy and in tip-top shape!

Regular Vet Check-ups

Just like we visit the doctor for check-ups, budgies need to see a special bird doctor called an avian veterinarian. These amazing veterinarians know all about budgies and how to keep them healthy. Regular check-ups are important to make sure our budgie is in good health.

The vet will check their feathers, beak, and overall well-being.

It's a fun adventure, and your budgie will feel loved and cared for!

Cleanliness and Hygiene

Budgies love to keep their feathers nice and clean, and it's our job to help them.

Keep their cage clean by removing any droppings and uneaten food every day. The water dish needs to be cleaned frequently. All the walls of it need to be rubbed with a soft sponge on the inside every day to prevent "biofilm" from forming. Only then will they have clean, fresh water to drink.

Once a week, give their cage a thorough clean, using mild soap and water. Rinse it well and let it dry completely before putting everything back.

This way, your budgie will have a fresh and tidy home to enjoy!

Exercise and Playtime

Budgies love to spread their wings and have a good stretch!

They need exercise and playtime every day to stay happy and healthy.

Take your budgie out of their cage for supervised playtime in a safe and budgie-proofed area.

You can let them fly around (make sure windows and doors are closed!) or set up a small budgie playground with toys and perches.

Playtime is a great way for you and your budgie to bond and have fun together!

Bonus Tip

Budgies also love to take baths! You can provide a shallow dish with lukewarm water for them to splash around and clean their feathers. It's like their own little spa day! To encourage your budgie to bathe, you can put a bit of grass or leaves into the dish. Never use soap or shampoo, as it would damage budgies natural coating of his feathers.

By taking care of your budgie's health, you're showing them love and ensuring they live a long and happy life. Regular vet check-ups, cleanliness, and hygiene, along with exercise and playtime, are the key ingredients to keeping your budgie healthy and thriving!

Now that you know how to keep your budgie in top shape, it's time to be their health champion!

Remember, if you ever have any concerns about your budgie's health or need advice, don't hesitate to consult with an adult or the avian veterinarian.

Together, we'll make sure our budgie friends are healthy and full of energy and joy!

Budgie School

Chapter 7

Budgie Loves Budgie School

Did you know that budgies love to learn? And they learn better when they like their teacher. Hey, that's YOU! So, let's become buddies and have lots of fun learning together.

Making Friends with My Budgie

To be a good budgie teacher, spend as much time around your feathery friend as you can.

For example, let him be next to you when you are studying - in his cage or out. It's better to have him in his cage if he's otherwise distracting you from homework.

At first, our budgie might be a little scared of us.

But don't worry, we can help them feel safe and loved.

The key to bonding is patience and kindness.

Treat budgie like you would treat a friend and respect his feelings. We need to be gentle and calm around our budgie.

No sudden movements or loud noises, as it might scare them. Instead, let's use soft and soothing voices to talk to them.

As our budgie begins to trust us, they'll feel more comfortable around us.

This is when their inner magic starts to show! They'll want to play and explore with us. When they feel safe and loved, they'll learn better and faster.

One way to win our budgie's heart is through tasty treats!

We can offer them yummy foods they love. When they see that we bring good things, they'll start to trust us more.

It's like sharing a special snack with a new friend.

They will also learn to understand the meaning of the tone of your voice, and they pay close attention to it being soft or loud.

Even though they don't know the meaning of your words they'll know if you're happy or not. And, of course, they really like it when you to praise them for being a good bird.

Teaching Budgie Cool Tricks

At budgie school, we get to teach our feathered pals some awesome tricks! We'll start with simple ones, like "step up" or "turn around." It's like a budgie dance party!

We repeat the trick slowly and give budgie time to understand. With practice and consistency, our budgie will become a superstar at performing tricks.

When your budgie does a trick correctly, give them a treat and show them how happy you are.

They'll be super excited to learn more tricks and make you proud.

Practice makes perfect, so let's have fun and keep trying together!

Rewarding Good Behaviour

At budgie school, we love positive reinforcement. That means we reward our budgies when they do something good. It's like giving them a big high-five!

When your budgie listens to you and does what you ask, give them a treat and lots of praise.

They'll feel happy and encouraged to keep doing their best.

Celebrate their small victories, and soon they'll be showing off their amazing skills!

In budgie school, we have a blast learning and growing together. Our friendship gets stronger, and our budgies become superstars.

So, let's spread our wings, have fun, and make budgie school the coolest place to be!

Remember, in budgie school, we build strong bonds of friendship.

It takes time and patience, but it's totally worth it.

With love and understanding, our budgie will become our best buddy and want to do fun things together!

Another Little Budgie Song

(to celebrate our glorious budgies)

To tame a bird, a tricky feat,
A patient heart, you must entreat.

With treats in hand,
you'll win their grace,
A little snack to tame their pace.

Their shyness gone,
their hearts will sing,
With love and trust,
they'll spread their wing.

So, bribe them with their favourite snack,
And watch them follow your sweet track!

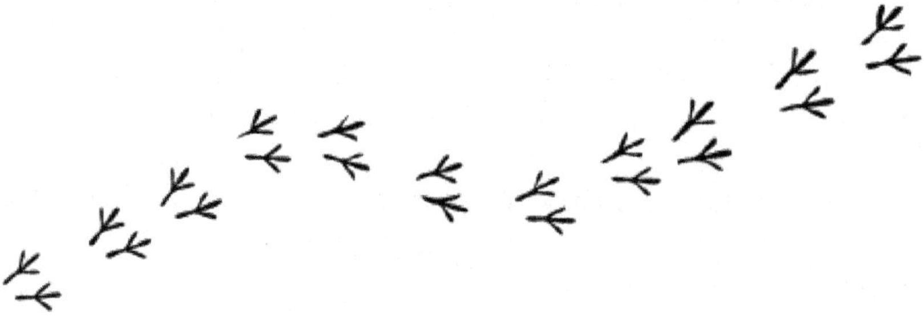

Chapter 8

Teaching Budgie Cool Tricks

In the last chapter, we talked about how much budgie likes going to school.

Now let's talk about how exactly we can teach our budgie a few cool tricks, shall we?

Remember, before we can teach budgie any tricks, we need to become friends and build trust with our budgie first. Slowly.

When your budgie has started to trust you, you can sometimes offer your budgie a treat from your hand, such as millet spray, a sunflower seed or a small piece of apple.

We should keep treats to training times only, then our budgie will know that the treat is a reward for good behaviour.

Trick No. 1 - Step Up

When budgie has learned that you offer them good things, they will like coming to you for treats and food.

Now is the time to teach budgie their first trick: STEP UP!

Hold the treat a little away from where budgie is sitting, but not too close, so they can't quite reach it. Now hold out a finger of your other hand, like a perch between budgie and your millet spray and say "Step Up"!

At first budgie might be scared, but give them some time and soon they'll be trying to reach the treat and step on your hand.

Hold your hands still and wait. You may have to do this a few times before budgie can overcome their natural fear. You are much bigger than them, and it will take time for them to take heart and go for the treat, so be patient.

If your budgie is very afraid of your hand, hold out a perch so they can hop on that first to come to you, and gradually they'll be less and less afraid. Repeat this trick often and always reward budgie with a treat for stepping up.

Note: Never try to 'grab' your budgie in it's cage, so they don't become afraid of your hands.

Trick No. 2 - Turn Around

This trick is very easy to teach.

Teach it after budgie has learned trick number 1 "Step Up".

Hold the millet spray or a small treat, such as a sunflower seed, slightly above budgies head. As they reach out to get the treat, slowly move the treat in a circular motion. Budgie will turn their head and then follow the treat.

Move it in a full circle to ask budgie to turn around and praise them generously when they do. Give them the treat (or a nibble of the millet spray) to reward them when they turn around fully.

Remember, budgie is likely to remember and repeat behaviours that get rewarded. So repeat these tricks often.

You can teach other similar tricks in the same way, such as "high five" or calling budgie to fly to you ("come here").

To get budgie to fly to you first teach "Step Up" then move a little further away from them and repeat the same as for "Step Up".

At first budgie will jump on your hand, then fly to your hand, as you move a little further away each time.

Chapter 9

Budgie's Chirpy Talks

In this chapter, we will explore the fascinating world of understanding budgie sounds, reading their body language, and the amazing talent of talking and mimicking.

Let's get started!

Budgies are incredibly vocal and expressive birds.

They use a variety of sounds and body language to communicate with their owners and other budgies.

Understanding what your budgie is trying to say is a rewarding part of building a strong bond with your feathered friend.

Understanding Budgie Sounds

Chirping

Chirping is the most common sound you'll hear from your budgie.
It's their way of expressing happiness and contentment. Sometimes, they'll chirp softly when they're feeling sleepy or relaxed.

Chattering

Chattering sounds are often heard when your budgie is excited or playful. It's their way of expressing joy and enthusiasm.

Singing

Budgies are natural songbirds. Male budgies, in particular, love to sing beautiful melodies to attract mates or simply to show off their singing skills.

Screeching

Loud screeching may show that your budgie is feeling frightened, anxious, or in pain. It's essential to check on them and ensure they're comfortable and safe.

Reading Budgie's Body Language

Fluffed Feathers: When your budgie fluffs up its feathers, it means they are trying to conserve body heat and might be feeling a bit chilly. If they sit like this for a longer time and are not as lively as usual, they may need a check-up with a vet.

Head Bobbing: A budgie bobbing its head is often a sign of curiosity, interest or excitement. They do this when investigating something new or when they want to play.

Puffed-out Cheeks: Puffed-out cheeks might indicate that your budgie is feeling threatened or annoyed. Be cautious not to stress them further in such situations.

Tail Wagging: If your budgie wags its tail from side to side, it is generally a sign of happiness and excitement.

Tail Bobbing: If your budgie is bobbing its tail up and down that is not such a good thing. If they are also fluffed up or listless or sleep a lot during the day, it's time for a visit to the vet!

Talking and Mimicking

Budgies are excellent mimics, and some can learn to talk!

Spend time talking to your budgie, and they might start picking up words and phrases from you.

Be patient when teaching your budgie to talk. Repeat words clearly and consistently, and reward them with treats or praise when they make an effort or "talk" to you.

Each budgie has its own personality, and not all of them like to talk. However, they will still communicate with you through chirps and body language.Remember, the more time you spend with your budgie, the better you'll understand its unique sounds and behaviours.

Be attentive and responsive to its needs, and your bond with your chirpy friend will grow stronger day by day.

Chapter 10

Budgie Loves to DANCE

My Budgie and Music

Meet my budgie Tango. He is very cute and special, and what's more: Tango loves to dance!

Did you know that budgies love music, just like we do?

When we play music, our budgies can listen and enjoy it too!

They might even start to chirp along. Different types of music can make budgies feel happy or calm.

So, let's explore how music can make our budgies feel good!

Budgie's Dance Moves

Have you ever seen your budgie move and groove?

Budgies are natural dancers! They have some cool dance moves. They might hop, sway, or even bob their heads. Sometimes they even spread their wings and wiggle their tails. It's so fun to watch them! It's so much fun to see the awesome dance moves budgies can do.

Enjoying Dance Time Together

Do you want to have a dance party with your budgie?

It's a great way to bond and have fun together! Choose some music that your budgie likes. You can try different songs and see which ones make your budgie move the most. My budgies love the song jingle bells, no matter what time of the year! Create a safe space for dancing, and join in the fun! You can dance and sing along with your budgie. It will make both of you happy!

In this chapter, we discovered that budgies love music and have their own special dance moves, and how to enjoy dance time together with our budgies.

So, put on some music, show off your dance moves, and have have a ball with your budgie!

A Little Poem about Tango

(my budgie who loves to dance!)

Meet Tango, my budgie, who, what is the chance!?

Loves Cha-cha and Rumba - Yes, he loves to dance!

Paso Doble, Waltz, Cha-Cha, he's roaming the floor

Spreading joy, fun and laughter - forever-more.

Tango, the budgie, full of grace, full of charm,

Loves to spin and to twirl, causing hearts to warm.

Oh Tango, oh budgie, oh dancer so fine,

Your talent and charm, they truly shine.

With every beat, you steal the show,

A feathered king of dance! Hello!

Now, let us join Tango, with cheerful sway,

And dance along, each as we may

For Tango, the budgie, taught us this:

That dancing and joy are the spirit's true bliss.

Chapter 11

Budgie's Social Life

In this chapter, we will explore the social life of budgies and how they interact with others.

Budgies are social birds and enjoy the company of their flock, which can include other budgies and even humans. Let's discover the wonderful world of budgie friendships!

Budgie Buddies and Flock Behaviour

Budgies are flock birds: Did you know that budgies love to be around their friends?

In the wild, budgies live together in big groups called flocks. They stick together and take care of each other, just like a big family. It's their natural way of living!

Flock behaviour: Budgies have their own special language to talk to each other. They chirp, tweet, and sing songs to communicate. When they want to show that they like someone, they groom and preen each other's feathers. It's like giving their friends a gentle tickle!

Hierarchy in the flock: In every flock, there is a leader or a boss budgie. This boss budgie helps make decisions and keeps everyone safe. Other budgies follow the boss budgie's lead. They have a special order in the flock, and they all know who is in charge!

Budgies are social creatures, and they love having friends.

They can make friends with other budgies and even with you! Just be patient, introduce them slowly, and watch their friendship blossom.

Enjoy the journey of building wonderful friendships with your budgie buddies!

How Budgie Makes Friends

Just like you, budgies can make friends too! They can become very close buddies with other budgies or even with humans. It's amazing how they can form such strong bonds with their friends.

Slow introductions: When budgies meet new friends, it's important to take things slowly. Budgies need time to get to know each other and feel comfortable. We can introduce them gradually, letting them spend time together and get acquainted. This way, they can become good friends step by step.

Signs of friendship: Budgies have special ways to show that they like someone. They show affection by preening each other's feathers, just like giving a little beauty touch-up.

When they like someone they sometimes tap on their beak to express affection, it's like when we put a hand on someone's shoulder.

They also share their yummy food and chirp happily together. These are all signs that they are becoming great friends!

Budgies thrive in a social environment, and understanding their social behaviour can help us provide them with a fulfilling and enriched life. By fostering friendships and engaging in interactive play, we can create a joyful social life for our budgies.

Remember, each budgie has its own unique personality, so observe and learn from your budgie to create a special bond that will last a lifetime. Enjoy the wonders of budgie socialization and have fun together!

Chapter 12

Adventures with My Budgie

Like humans, budgies love a good adventure. And they also like playing outdoors and being in the sunshine when the weather is nice. Let's see what we need to know about keeping them safe during outdoor adventures.

Outdoor Playtime Care

It's so exciting for your budgie to go on outdoor adventures! But before you take your budgie anywhere, there are a few things to keep in mind to keep your budgie safe.

Choose a safe area

When playing outside, make sure you find a safe and secure space for your budgie. It should be an enclosed area where your budgie can't fly away or be harmed by other animals. If you want to take their cage outside into the sunshine on a nice day, find a spot that you can keep an eye on, because.... you better:

Watch out for predators

What are some creatures out there you can think of who might see your budgie as a tasty snack?!

Yes, that's right!

Keep a close eye on your budgie and make sure there are no cats, dogs, rats, falcons, butcher birds or other predators around.

What about snakes, crocodiles or dragons?

Avoid extreme weather

Budgies are sensitive to changes in temperature. Let's not play outside on very hot, windy or cold days.

Find a comfortable time when the weather is just right for both you and your budgie.

On sunny days always make sure budgie can move into the shade whenever it wants to.

Traveling with Budgie

Preparing for a trip

If you're going on a trip and want to take your budgie with you, there are a few things to plan and prepare beforehand.

73

Secure the travel cage

When travelling, make sure your budgie is in a sturdy and secure travel cage. It should have enough space for your budgie to move comfortably but be safe enough to prevent any escapes.

Bring familiar items

To help your budgie feel more at ease during the journey, bring some familiar items from home, like their favourite toys or something else from their every day cage. This will provide them with a sense of security and familiarity.

Keep the environment calm

When traveling, try to keep the environment as calm and peaceful as possible. Loud noises or sudden movements can startle your budgie. Keep them in a quiet area and play soft, soothing music to help them relax. Keep them at the right temperature at all times and away from drafts.

Exploring New Environments

Budgies are curious creatures and love to explore new environments!

If you're taking your budgie to a new place, introduce it slowly and gradually. Let them get used to the sights, sounds, and smells at their own pace.

Watch for hazards

When exploring new places, be aware of any potential hazards that could harm your budgie.

Keep an eye out for toxic plants, open windows or doors, drafts, and other dangers that they might encounter, such as spiders, wild birds, rodents or crocodiles (!?).

Provide a safe space

Set up a safe area in the new environment where your budgie can retreat to if they feel overwhelmed. It could be a small cage or a cosy corner with their favourite toys and perches. This will give them a sense of security and comfort. When budgie seems nervous or scared cover a part of its cage so it can feel safe.

Adventures with your budgie can be so much fun! Just remember to take precautions, plan ahead, and make sure your budgie feels safe and comfortable during your adventures together.

Enjoy exploring new places and creating wonderful memories with your feathered friend!

Chapter 13

Goodnight Budgie

Just as for humans, sleep is very important for budgies. In nature, budgies sleep from sunset to sunrise. We should allow budgie to do the same when living with humans.

Ideally, budgie should sleep around 12 hours each night.

Creating a Calm Environment

Preparing for bedtime

Exactly like us, budgies need a calm and peaceful environment to get a good night's sleep. Let's create a cosy and soothing space for your budgie.

Dim the lights

Before bedtime, dim the lights in the room to create a relaxing atmosphere. This helps signal to your budgie that it's time to wind down.

Reduce noise

Keep the noise level low around your budgie's sleeping area. Avoid loud conversations, television volume, or any other noisy activities that may disturb their sleep, like beeps and bangs.

Bedtime Routines

Establish a routine: Budgies thrive on routines, and having a bedtime routine can help them feel secure and ready for sleep. While budgies don't need to brush their teeth it can be nice for them if you speak to them softly each night before bed; my budgie bubbles has learned to say "Night, night" and looks forward to a little chat each evening.

Cover the cage: Budgies are more comfortable sleeping in a covered cage. Use a soft, breathable cover to create a cosy and dark space for your budgie to rest.

Provide a comfortable perch: Make sure your budgie has a comfortable perch to sleep on. Opt for a natural wooden perch that allows them to relax their feet and get a good night's sleep.

Bedtime bonding: Before covering the cage, spend some quiet time with your budgie. Talk to them softly and offer gentle pets or head scratches if they enjoy them. This helps strengthen your bond and lets your budgie know they are loved.

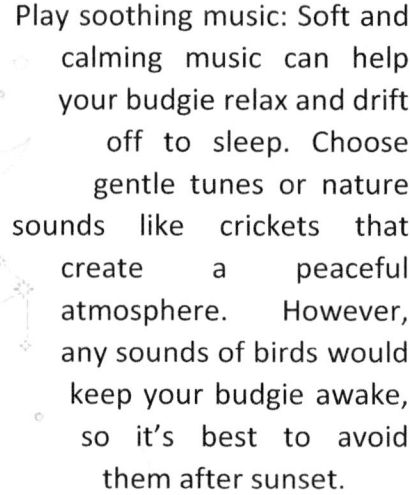

Play soothing music: Soft and calming music can help your budgie relax and drift off to sleep. Choose gentle tunes or nature sounds like crickets that create a peaceful atmosphere. However, any sounds of birds would keep your budgie awake, so it's best to avoid them after sunset.

Goodnight wishes: Before you say goodnight to your budgie, give them a gentle kiss or a loving word. My budgie Happy loves to say "Good Night"

Let them know it's time to rest and have sweet dreams.

Remember, budgies need plenty of sleep to stay healthy and happy. By creating a calm environment, establishing bedtime routines, and showing your budgie love and care before sleep, you're helping them have a restful night.

Goodnight, Budgie! Sleep tight and have the sweetest dreams, knowing that you are safe and loved in your cosy home.

Final Chapter

Does My Budgie Dream?

It's a fascinating question, isn't it?!

While we can't know for sure what goes on in their little birdy minds, scientists believe that budgies may indeed dream while they sleep.

Just like us, budgies have an active mind that processes experiences and memories. When they're fast asleep, their brains may be busy creating all sorts of interesting and exciting dream adventures.

So, what do you think budgie might be dreaming about? Maybe they dream of soaring through the sky, exploring vast landscapes, or even having fun with their human friends.

It's so much fun to imagine the magical and whimsical dreams that budgies could have!

Next time you see your budgie peacefully snoozing, you can wonder if they're off on an exciting dream journey. Just remember to let them sleep peacefully and not disturb their dreams. Budgies need their rest to stay healthy and happy.

Remember, dreams are a special part of our sleep, and they add a touch of magic to our lives.

Who knows, maybe one day your budgie will share their dreams with you in their own special way. Until then, let them enjoy a peaceful slumber and have wonderful dreams!

Sweet dreams, little budgie!

84

APPENDIX
Things I Do For My Budgie Every Day

(because of love!)

Morning	During the Day	At Sunset
After sunrise: Enjoy happy budgie Good Morning chirpies	Spend time with budgie	Remove water from cage and clean water containers
Give healthy breakfast vegetables, seeds or pellets (dry, soaked or sprouted seed and sometimes fruit, if budgie likes it)	Play with budgie or teach tricks	Clean out bottom of cage and remove uneaten foods
Give clean water	Give treats for courageous or good behavior	Cover cage and ensure budgie has a peaceful sleep
Talk with budgie	Play music or radio that is happy and calming for budgie	
	Check on food/water and replace or refill when needed	

What Did You Think of My Budgie Loves to Dance?

Dear Friend of Budgies and Books,

First of all, thanks a million for reading this book! I, along with all the budgies in the world that live in people's homes, am super grateful to you!

I hope this book brought you lots of joy and fun, and if it did, it would be awesome if you could share it with your friends too! They'll love learning about budgies just like you did!

If you enjoyed the book and found it helpful, I'd love to hear from you. You can leave a review on *Amazon*, and it will really help me become a better writer for my future books.

Remember, your feedback is essential to me, so I'm counting on you!

Wishing you and your budgie flock all the best! Keep reading and exploring the world of budgies!

With love and feathers,

Nicole Soham

Printed in Dunstable, United Kingdom

65190673R00050